SMART ANIMALS

BRILLIANT BIRDS

Thanks to the creative team:

Senior Editor: Alice Peebles
Fact checking: Kate Mitchell
Design: www.collaborate.agency

First published in Great Britain in 2016
by Hungry Tomato Ltd
PO Box 181
Edenbridge
Kent, TN8 9DP

Copyright © 2016 Hungry Tomato Ltd

No part of this publication may be reproduced, stored in a retrieval system, or transmitted in any form or by any means, electronic, mechanical, photocopying, recording, or otherwise, without the prior written permission of the copyright owner.

A CIP catalogue record for this book is available from the British Library.

ISBN 978-1-910684-54-2

Printed and bound in China

Discover more at
www.hungrytomato.com

SMART ANIMALS

BRILLIANT BIRDS

BY JOHN FARNDON
ILLUSTRATED BY CRISTINA PORTOLANO

CONTENTS

SMART BIRDS	6
CLEVER!	8
GETTING THE MESSAGE	10
DETECTOR POWER	12
I HEAR YOU	14
SUPER SENSES	16
VANISHING ACTS	18
BRILLIANT BUILDERS	20
TOOL USERS	22
MARVELLOUS MIMICS	24
JOURNEY BIRDS	26
THE BEST OF THE BEST	28
SPECIAL SKILLS	30
INDEX	32

SMART BIRDS

If you ever get called 'bird brain' you should take it as a compliment. Despite their small size, some birds are very, very clever indeed. And they have special skills and characteristics that help them to survive.

First, here's a taster of just how amazing birds are, before we even get on to the really clever stuff....

SAVANNA SPEEDSTERS

Although the fastest creature on land is the cheetah, which can reach 120.7 km/h (75 mph), the supercharged ostrich (left) is not so far behind. It can't fly, but its giant legs whirl it along at up to nearly 100 km/h (60 mph)! In the time it takes the world's best athlete to run a kilometre, an ostrich could run four. Byee!

BIG BIRDS

The ostrich is also the largest living bird. It grows up to 2.7 m (9 ft) tall and can weigh more than 156 kg (344 lb). But the ostrich is too heavy to fly. The largest flying bird is the wandering albatross (below). Its wings stretch out 3.5 m (11 ft 6 in). The heaviest flying birds are bustards.

THAT'S FLYING

The fastest flier is the peregrine falcon (right), which can reach astonishing speeds when stooping - diving on its prey with its wings tucked in. Some falcons have been recorded at speeds of 389 km/h (242 mph). But swifts are the fastest in level flight, with the white-throated needletail flashing along at 169 km/h (105 mph).

WINGING IT

Terns are astonishing for their long flights. In fact, some almost never land. After leaving its nesting grounds as a youngster, the sooty tern (left) remains aloft for up to 10 years, only landing on water from time to time. Scientists once recorded a common tern flying more than 26,000 km (16,000 miles) from Finland to Australia, covering 200 km (125 miles) every day.

OLD BIRDS

In 2014, a flamingo called Greater had to be put to sleep because it was suffering from rheumatism. Greater was 83 years old! Flamingoes (right) are not the only birds that can live into their 80s. Parrots and albatrosses can, too. Cookie, a Major Mitchell's cockatoo in Chicago's Brookfield Zoo, was nearly 83 in 2016.

CLEVER!

Folk tales often tell how crows and their relatives, the rooks, are clever tricksters. But scientists thought these were just stories – until they started doing experiments. Then they found that these birds are very clever indeed. In fact, they're cleverer than most of us are by the age of seven! So don't try and trick a crow.

DINNER'S UP

Long ago, Ancient Greek storyteller Aesop told a fable about a crow dropping stones into a narrow jug so that the water rose and it could drink. Scientists tested this story by putting a tempting worm on a cork at the bottom of a deep jar. Sure enough, all the rooks in the test dropped stones into the jar, raising the water level and getting the worm.

LET THAT BE A LESSON

To teach visitors the importance of looking after litter, staff at the Montecasino Bird Garden in Johannesburg, South Africa, tried an experiment. They trained crows to pick up litter and drop it in a dustbin. The crows proved very good at the job!

ROOKS RULE

Rooks and their relatives are very social birds. In winter, they often gather to roost (sleep) in large colonies in the treetops known as rookeries.

THE TOOL FOR THE JOB

Most scientists think that using tools shows an animal is really clever. The crows of the Pacific islands of New Caledonia are perhaps the cleverest tool users of all. These crows don't just use a stick to get insects out of holes in trees. They first bend the end of the stick into a hook, so it works even better at poking out insects.

GETTING THE MESSAGE

Many animals have distinctive calls. But apart from humans and whales, birds are the only ones that sing. A song is not a single sound, but a tune that goes up and down in a particular pattern like music. Birds usually sing early in the morning. They sing to attract a mate or to declare their territory. Outside the tropics, it is mostly male birds that sing.

THE LARK RISING

The best singers are songbirds, such as warblers, sparrows, blackbirds and robins. And the most loved songbird is the skylark (above). Other birds sing while perching, but the skylark soars up into the sky as it pours out a glorious, very complex blizzard of notes.

ROOTS MUSIC

Male kakapos of New Zealand don't so much sing as blow their own trumpets. To attract a female, they inflate air sacs in their chest to help make a long trumpeting sound, mixed in with high 'chings'. They cannot fly, so they dig out a bowl in the ground and sing from that.

BOOM TIME

The bittern's call is not exactly beautiful. But it's certainly effective and often haunting to hear in the lonely marshes that are its home. The low, booming sound carries more than 5 km (3 miles) away on a still night.

SINGING DUELS

Marsh wrens don't always sing by themselves. Sometimes a male will engage in a singing duel with another male. This is isn't just a battle to see who can sing loudest. It's an elaborate duet. One bird takes the lead vocal line, and the other slots his tune in between, like a beautiful counter melody.

THEIR OWN MUSIC

Most birds don't just have one song that they repeat over and over, but a whole repertoire of phrases that they mix up. The brown thrasher has as many different phrases as we have words! A century ago, bird expert F. Schuyler Mathews wrote some down as music. Near right is an example of a brown thrasher song.

SINGING MACHINE

Birds sing so well because they make their song deep inside. They don't have vocal cords near the top of the throat like us. Instead, they make the song when their breath goes out through a Y-shaped pipe called the syrinx, just above their lungs. The syrinx has two branches, so they can sing two notes at once.

DETECTOR POWER

Most birds rely on sharp eyesight to navigate and find food. But not oilbirds and swiftlets. They sleep in dark caves by day and fly only at night in dense forests. These birds have their very own super sense – an echolocation system as good as any bat's.

SOUND SYSTEM

Echolocation works using sound. Oilbirds and swiftlets send out a stream of audible clicks. The clicks bounce off objects and echo back to the birds, showing them where things are. Swiftlets use echolocation to catch flying insects.

Swiftlet

Insect

)) = Clicks from bird

)) = Sound waves echoing back from insect

ECHO SENSE

Oilbirds live in northern South America and eat fruit. They have specially adapted eyes that help them to see well in twilight. This enables them to find food at dusk and dawn. But they use echolocation to find their way round the pitch dark caves where they sleep during the day, and avoid bumping into each other!

OPEN WIDE

Like swiftlets, nightjars fly in the dark and catch insects by 'hawking' – gulping them down in mid-air. But nightjars don't use echolocation. Instead their big eyes help them to see at dusk and dawn when they hunt – and their beak can open so wide they're much less likely to miss!

BIRD'S NEST SOUP

Just like the oilbird, the swiftlets of southern Asia and Indonesia sleep in caves and fly at night. They eat insects, not fruit, though. Their nests in caves are made mostly of their own gooey saliva. Chinese people gather these nests by climbing long poles and cook them in water to make bird's nest soup.

GUACHÁRO CAVE

Oilbirds live in huge colonies, clinging to the walls of their caves with tiny, hooklike feet. They got their name because long ago oilbird chicks were caught and boiled down to make oil. The most famous oilbird colony is Guacháro Cave in Venezuela, home to over 15,000 oilbirds. Their name is *guacháro* in Spanish.

I HEAR YOU

The real deadly assassins of the night are owls, and especially barn owls. When they go out hunting at night, they are looking for mice, voles, rats and even rabbits. They spot their prey in dark with their amazing eyes and even more amazing hearing.

OWL FACE

Unlike many birds', owl's eyes face forwards. This means that both eyes work together to help them judge distance as ours do. The special cone-like shape of each cheek focuses light and sound towards the owl's ears and eyes. Barn owls' eyes aren't quite as big as those of other species, and may not be as good for hunting at night, but they are backed by the best hearing of any tested.

BEHIND YOU!

An owl's eyes have a fairly narrow angle of vision. But this helps to keep their eyesight super-sharp. The owl can also see in any direction simply by turning its head. Its neck is so flexible it can rotate its head to face backwards!

SUPER HEARING

A recent experiment by scientists with a barn owl in a vast, pitch dark room showed the owl can pinpoint a mouse by sound alone. We can work out direction because we have two ears. This means that if a sound is not straight ahead, it reaches one ear slightly earlier than the others. Barn owls pinpoint sounds in the same way, but much better because their hearing is so acute.

OFFSET EARS

A barn owl's earholes are slightly offset – slightly higher on one side than the other. This means that when they are flying along face down, sounds reach one ear marginally ahead of the other. This is why their directional sense of sound is so uncannily accurate.

GHOSTLY WINGS

Some people find barn owls eery because they fly silently on great, white, ghostly wings. But any noise would alert their prey and disrupt the precise hearing they need to track targets. Their silent flight depends on special features in the wings, such as soft, downy feathers that don't rub together, and soft noise-damping fringes on the wing tips.

SUPER SENSES

With high-tech cameras, we can see things clearly at great distances. But to the eagle, that comes naturally. It has the animal world's sharpest eyes. It can see clearly as far as 80 km (50 miles) away – five times further than we can.

SHARP EYES

An eagle's huge eyes let in a lot of light. They are also five times more densely packed with receptors than ours - like a camera with mega pixels. The lens changes shape more quickly than ours, to keep things in focus. Even the fovea (the receptor structure at the centre of each eye) is much deeper than ours, making them like telephoto lenses. Eagles see more colours, too!

HIGH HOMES

Eagles' nests are called eyries. Golden eagles like to make their eyries high up on steep cliff faces. That keeps their eggs entirely safe from most predators. But it means the only way out for the young chicks is to learn to fly straight away!

PANORAMIC VIEW

Because eagle's eyes are on the sides of the head, they can see almost all the way round, giving them a panoramic view. And yet, unlike most birds (apart from owls and other birds of prey), their eyes face partly forwards so that the view from each one overlaps. The slightly different view from each eye enables the eagle to judge distances, like us. This is called binocular vision.

LIFTING POWER

An eagle doesn't have strong jaws like a big cat or wolf. But it has sharp talons and a razor-sharp beak that can be just as deadly for prey. The talons are also amazingly strong. An eagle can grab a heavy victim in its talons and fly with it back to its nest. A golden eagle can carry a dog or even a small deer in its talons.

EAGLE HUNTING

Golden eagles are the least tame animals you can imagine. Yet 2,000 years ago or more, Kazakh people learned to train these eagles to hunt red foxes. Training eagles takes many years. The Kazakhs call those who hunt with eagles *bürkitshi*, and most of them now live in Mongolia.

VANISHING ACTS

Many birds are masters of the art of vanishing to avoid birds of prey. Their drab plumage provides the perfect camouflage when seen from above, blending almost invisibly into the surroundings. Birds that sleep or forage on the ground in the daytime, nesting females and young chicks all need to be particularly well-camouflaged.

NOT STANDING OUT

Most birds rely on the colours and patterns in their feathers to avoid being seen. But the bittern uses another kind of camouflage. When it's among tall reeds, it sticks its neck and beak up high in the air so that it takes on the shape of the reeds. That makes it surprisingly hard to see from a distance. This is called 'posture camouflage'.

SNOW BLIND

To be effective, camouflage has to match a bird's surroundings. So the brown colours that suit forest birds are no good for Arctic birds, where dark colours would show up against the snow. That's why, unlike every other owl, the snowy owl has brilliant white plumage that makes it merge into the Arctic snow – not just for predators, but for the owl's own prey.

KEEPING MUM

Mother birds are very vulnerable while they sit on the nest waiting for eggs to hatch. So most females have drab, mottled patterns to avoid being seen. Ground-nesting birds, such as ducks, are especially at risk. If a predator comes near, the mother duck will sit tight on her nest until the last minute, before exploding into the air to draw attention away from her eggs.

TAKING A LEAF

During the day, nightjars rest on the ground where they are open to attack, not just by birds of prey, but by four-legged hunters as well. So they need to be very well-camouflaged. They usually lie down amid leaf litter, where their indistinct brown colouring makes them really hard to see.

THE DISAPPEARING POTOO

Few birds are better at camouflage than the common potoo of Central and South America. It flies at night to hunt insects, like its close relative the nightjar. But during the day, it perches on tree stumps, and is disguised to look like part of the stump. If danger threatens, it freezes completely, looking just like a broken branch.

BRILLIANT BUILDERS

Like us, some birds are great home builders. While many birds just lay their eggs in a hole on the ground, some construct proper nests. Each species has its own distinctive nest, from the neat cup of a blackbird to the sewn-up leaf of the tailorbird. But no birds have nests as elaborate as weaver birds'.

After creating a ring, the weaver pulls the grass around the outside

He leans back to pull the grass back through

Then he folds the end and threads it through the ring

The bird perches on the ring as he knots the grass

WEAVING A NEST

Weaver birds skilfully weave twigs together with their beaks to make sturdy nests. They are so-called because they are very good at this. The master of them all is the baya weaver of India. Its nest is like a hanging basket. The male makes it from grass and the leaves of paddy rice, tying them all together with complex knots and stitches.

DESIGNER NEST

Male satin bowerbirds of Australia make some of the flashiest nests of any bird. Their nests have roofs, which is why they are called bowers. The bird also strews brightly coloured objects across the entrance to impress females – red flowers, blue stones, bits of coloured plastic, and much more.

BIRD TOWN

Sociable weaver birds live in southern Africa and live up to their name. They construct a huge, intricate town of nests attached to trees and poles, the most spectacular structures built by any bird. Pairs of birds have their own nests within the town, but they all work together to create a home for 100 or more pairs. Living together like this means that one of the birds can be on the lookout for danger.

ART OF THE NEST

Ruby-throated hummingbirds come from the south to spend the summer in eastern North America. They build beautiful little nests. The female starts by knotting spider silk round a tree branch to anchor it, and weaves together bark, leaf strands and more silk to create a tiny cup Then she carefully lines it with fur or feathers for warmth. Finally, she decorates the outside with green lichen for camouflage.

TOOL USERS

Crows are not the only birds to use tools. In fact, many more birds can use tools than you might think, including woodpecker finches, vultures, nuthatches and macaws. Birds can't hold tools in their hands, but their beaks do the trick.

EGG CRACKER

Ostrich eggs are so tough that the Egyptian vulture finds them hard to crack. So the vulture picks up a stone and flings it at the egg again and again until it smashes. Ravens are even cleverer, though. They give an egg to a vulture to smash. Then, when the vulture has done the hard work, the ravens pair up to drive off the vulture and take the egg themselves.

NUTCRACKERS

Nuts are hard to eat, even for a bird with a beak as tough as the hyacinth macaw. The nut slips away as the bird tries to bite it. So the clever macaw wraps chewed leaf around the nut to hold it in place, or even uses a makeshift vice made of bits of wood.

GETTING UNDER THE BARK

Brown-headed nuthatches live in the pine forests of Louisiana. They're so small it's easy to think they can't be that clever. But the little nuthatches have been seen using chisels made from flakes of bark. They chisel away with these at the bark of a tree to get at the insects underneath. The birds are not strong, though, so it only works where the bark is quite flaky.

WHO NEEDS A DRILL?

Woodpecker finches live on the Galapagos islands. They are not woodpeckers at all but, like woodpeckers, can dig out insects from trees. While woodpeckers drill a hole, woodpecker finches probe for insects with a cactus spine or twig. Recently, woodpecker finches found some blackberry twigs and stripped away all the thorns except a few at the end – a perfect barbed probe.

MARVELLOUS MIMICS

Birds can make a wide range of sounds and be amazing mimics. The crow family, parrots, myna birds, bowerbirds, mockingbirds and thrashers are the best at doing impressions. Older birds especially may have a repertoire of thousands of sounds.

ALEX (ANIMAL LEARNING EXPERIMENT)

Alex the African grey was a very famous talking parrot. He was trained to talk by animal psychologist Irene Pepperburg for over 30 years. Before this experiment, scientists thought that birds could only mimic. But Alex learned more than 100 words and seemed to understand them, putting them together in different ways to say something new.

KEY UNDERSTANDING

Pepperburg showed that Alex the parrot didn't just copy words but had some idea what they meant. For example, he always said "Key" when he was shown a key – no matter what shape, size or colour it was. And if he was given a nut when he said, "I wanna banana", he'd sulk and ask for a banana again – sometimes even throwing the nut back to the researcher first!

GOODBYE

Sadly, Alex the parrot died quite young, at just 31 years old in 2007. But his last words to Irene Pepperburg were, "You be good, see you tomorrow. I love you."

PARROT-FASHION

The best talking birds of all are parrots. There are countless tales of parrots and their way with words. People use the term 'parrot-fashion' to describe mindless learning, though. The idea is that parrots can only mimic humans, without ever understanding words.

COPY CATS

The best bird mimics are the lyrebirds of Australia. They are famous for their spectacular tails and their astonishing vocal abilities. Usually they mimic the sounds of other birds, but those raised in captivity can mimic chainsaws, radios, camera shutters, car alarms and other man-made sounds with startling accuracy.

MYNAH DETAILS

Mynah birds are small, black birds related to starlings. They are often kept as pets and astonish people with their ability to mimic human speech, learning many words and phrases. One mynah, known as Kaleo, formed a strong bond with a dog called Jack. After Jack died, Kaleo kept saying, "I love Jack," and asking where he was.

JOURNEY BIRDS

Birds make the most astonishing journeys of any animal. Some, such as the wandering albatross, are on the move all the time. But the most epic journeys are migrations, as birds fly to warmer regions to escape the winter, or return to places where there is more food in summer. The greatest annual migrations are made by waders and seabirds.

THE FLIGHT RECORD

Each year wading birds called bar-tailed godwits migrate from Alaska to New Zealand. In 2007, a godwit was recorded flying 11,500 km (7,145 miles) from Alaska to New Zealand nonstop over the Pacific Ocean. That's the longest nonstop flight ever recorded. Amazingly, it took just nine days, so the little bird was flying nearly 1,300 km (800 miles) every day!

Jet aircraft 9,000 m/30,000 ft
Some cranes and swans 10,000 m/33,000 ft
Ruppell's vulture 11,300 m/37,000 ft
Mt. Everest
Alpine chough 8,000 m/26,500 ft
Bar-headed goose 89,900 m/29,500 ft
Songbirds 1,200 m/4,000 ft
Ducks and geese 1,500 m/5,000 ft
Bald eagle 3,000 m/10,000 ft

HIGH-FLIERS

Sometimes, birds encounter high mountain ranges across their migration path. Sometimes, the winds that blow in the right direction are high up. To cross mountains or catch winds, birds can reach impressive heights. Migrating birds start off low, then gradually fly higher and higher. The highest flier is Ruppell's vulture of northern Africa, which has been seen at 11,300 m (37,000 ft).

TERN AGAIN

The Arctic Tern makes the greatest migration of all. Late every summer, this small bird heads south from the Arctic. It flies round the world to Antarctica to catch summer there. Four or so months later, it flies all the way back for the Arctic summer. The round trip is an incredible 70,000 km (43,000 miles). On the way north, it flies over 520 km (320 miles) every day.

NORTHERN PROMISE

Compared to a tern, the northern wheatear is tiny. Yet it, too, makes an astonishingly long journey. It weighs barely 25 g (0.8 oz) but it makes a round trip of more than 30,000 km (18,640 miles). Every spring, it flies all the way from the Sahara fringes in Africa to the Arctic, crossing deserts and mountains on the way. This is the greatest journey by any songbird.

GOOSE AIR FORCE

The migrations of geese are one of the wonders of the natural world. They are all large birds, and they fly together in large flocks. Many fly in a V-formation. This helps the birds stay together and it saves energy as the front birds shelter the birds behind, which is why they take turns to fly in front.

27

THE BEST OF THE BEST

THE CROW FAMILY
SPECIES: 120
LIVE IN: Most places, except for the poles and the tip of South America
EAT: Insects, bugs, worms and fruit

Known by scientists as corvids, the crow family includes ravens, rooks, jackdaws, jays and magpies. They are very clever, medium to large birds.

SONGBIRDS
SPECIES: 4,000
LIVE IN: Everywhere but the poles
EAT: Mostly seeds, fruits, nectar, insects, small birds and small lizards

Known by scientists as passerines, or perching birds, songbirds include warblers, sparrows, blackbirds and robins.

SWIFTS
SPECIES: 100
LIVE IN: Most places but the polar extremes and deserts
EAT: Mostly flying insects

Swifts are among the fastest flying birds of all. Many have a characteristic forked tail and long swept-back wings.

BARN OWLS
SPECIES: 16
LIVE IN: Most places but the Sahara, parts of Asia and North America
EAT: Small mammals, such as mice and voles

Barn owls are one of the two families of owls. They have large heads and a characteristically heart-shaped face.

EAGLES
SPECIES: More than 60
LIVE IN: Three-quarters live in Eurasia and Africa
EAT: Small to medium mammals and fish

Eagles are big birds of prey with huge hooked beaks for tearing flesh, strong muscular legs and powerful talons.

POTOOS AND NIGHTJARS
SPECIES: More than 100
LIVE IN: Most places, except for the far north and south, and the Sahara
EAT: Flying insects

Potoos and nightjars are nocturnal birds that catch flying insects in their gaping mouths.

WEAVERBIRDS
SPECIES: 110
LIVE IN: Southern Africa and India
EAT: Seeds

Weaverbirds are so-called because they all weave elaborate nests. There may be as many as 10 billion of one species, the red-billed quelea.

TANAGERS
SPECIES: 240
LIVE IN: Tropical America
EAT: Anything, especially fruit, seeds, nectar and flower parts

The tanagers are a large class of finches. They include the Galapagos island finches known as Darwin's finches, which include woodpecker finches.

LYREBIRDS
SPECIES: 2
LIVE IN: Australia
EAT: Insects, bugs and worms

Lyrebirds are known for the spectacular tail feathers of the male, and for their amazing skill at mimicry.

TERNS
SPECIES: More than 50
LIVE IN: Everywhere
EAT: Fish

Terns are medium-sized seabirds. They are expert at diving for fish and great fliers, often covering long distances to reach breeding grounds.

SPECIAL SKILLS

As with the animals featured in this book, there are many that have a skill that's so special and so much more amazing than anything we could do, that you just have to say it's smart. Just being able to fly, of course, is a special skill that most birds have. But they have others, too.

SOARING AND GLIDING

Some birds glide on the air, barely flapping their wings. This saves a lot of energy, and helps them to stay aloft much longer. The best gliders are often large birds, such as the albatross, condor (left), vulture and eagle, which can glide for ages, scanning for prey. Some birds use rising currents of air to soar higher with no effort.

DIVING DEEP

Birds are not only good at flying. Penguins and many other birds are excellent swimmers, too. And a number of seabirds are remarkable divers, plunging deep into the sea in pursuit of fish. The deepest diver is Brünnich's guillemot (right). This bird, also known as the thick-billed murre, has been recorded making a dive of 210 m (690 ft), going down 2 m/sec (6.5 ft).

MIGHTY GRIP

Birds of prey have a remarkably strong grip, and their talons are long and vicious. Those of the harpy eagle (left) crunch together with a force of that's nine times as much as the average man's grip – and quite a lot more crushing than the bite of a wolf or a bear. That's why the harpy eagle can scrunch the skull of a monkey to a pulp.

CRASH-TESTED

Even the best diver has to be very careful to avoid injury when hitting the water. A gannet (right) smashes into the water much, much faster when diving for fish – with no ill effects. That's because its skull is reinforced like a built-in crash helmet. It also has built-in airbags in its neck and shoulders that can be inflated to cushion the impact. This means it can hit the water so fast – 145 km/h (90 mph) or more – that fish are knocked out by the impact.

JUST SWALLOW

The tawny frogmouth (left) doesn't bother to hunt. It just sits perfectly still and waits for dinner to jump into its mouth – which it does. Because the frogmouth is camouflaged to look like a tree stump, small birds, frogs and lizards venture close without realizing there's any danger. But if they do come too near, the frogmouth opens its gaping mouth, snaps it shut and swallows the victim whole in a fraction of a second.

INDEX

A
albatrosses 6
Arctic terns 27

B
bar-tailed godwit 26
barn owls 14, 15, 28
birdsong 10–11
bitterns 10, 18
bowerbirds 20
brown-headed nuthatch 23
brown thrashers 11
Brünnich's guillemot 30

C
crows 8, 9, 28

D
diving 30, 31
ducks 19

E
eagles 16, 17, 28, 31
echolocation 12

G
gannets 31
geese 27
golden eagles 16, 17

H
harpy eagles 31

K
kakapos 10

L
lyrebirds 25, 29

M
macaws 22
marsh wrens 10
mynah birds 25

N
nest building 20, 21
nightjars 12, 19, 29
northern wheatear 27

O
oilbirds 12, 13
ostrich 6
owls 14, 15, 18, 28

P
parrots 7, 22, 24, 25
peregrine falcon 7
potoos 19, 29

R
raven 22
rooks 9
ruby-throated hummingbird 21

S
skylark 10
snowy owl 18
song making 10–11
songbirds 10–11, 28
swiftlets 12
swifts 7, 28

T
tanagers 29
tawny frogmouth 31
terns 7, 27, 29
tools 8, 9, 22, 23

V
vultures 22, 26

W
weaver birds 20, 21, 29
woodpecker finch 23

THE AUTHOR

John Farndon is Royal Literary Fellow at Anglia Ruskin University in Cambridge, UK, and the author of a huge number of books for adults and children on science, technology and nature, including international best-sellers. He has been shortlisted four times for the Royal Society's Young People's Book Prize.

THE ILLUSTRATOR

Cristina Portolano was born in Naples, Italy, and studied in Bologna and Paris, graduating in Comics and Illustration. Her artwork has appeared in Italian magazines and comic books such as *Delebile* and *Teiera*. She lives and works in Bologna, and her first book has recently been published by Topipittori.

Picture Credits (abbreviations: t = top; b = bottom; c = centre; l = left; r = right)
© www.shutterstock.com:

2 cl, 6 cl, 6 bl, 7 tr, 7 cl, 7 br, 9 tr, 10 bl, 13 tr, 14 bl, 17 bl, 19 cr, 20 br, 21 tr, 22 br, 24 tl, 27 BL, 30 tl, 30 br, 31 tl, 31 cr, 31 bl, 32 cr.